A FOETAL HEART

Edward Lee

Acknowledgements are due to the editors of the following print and online magazines where some of these poems appeared:

Adelaide Literary Magazine, Allegro Poetry Journal, A New Ulster, A Thin Slice Of Anxiety, Better Than Starbucks, Bindweed, The Blue Nib, Cajun Mutt Press, cc&d Magazine, Constellate, Dreich Mag, The Echelon Review, Evening Street Review, Fixator Press, Flights, The High Window, Home Planet News, Iceberg Tales, The Incubator, Impspired, Linden Avenue Literary Journal, London Grip, Lothlorien Poetry Journal, North Of Oxford, One Art, Orchard Lea Books, Orson's Review, Praxis Magazine, Poetry Breakfast, Qutub Minar Review, Red Weather, Riggwelter, Ruddlerless Mariner, Sage Cigarettes, Scissor Tail Quarterly, Selcouth Station, The Seventh Quarry, Skylight 47, Snakeskin, Sparks Of Calliope, Synchronized Chaos, Thanks Hun, Toasted Cheese Literary, Trouvaille Review, Verbal Art

ISBN: 9798837135309

for Barry, for keeping me alive even when I didn't want him to

"THERE YOU ARE"

We kiss until we forget ourselves,
becoming strangers searching
for other strangers,
rediscover ourselves
as lips and tongues
continue to collide,
feel ourselves reborn
on the air we breathe into each other,
our eyes opening
as we pause,
whisper "there you are, oh
there you are".

LIVING

Soft to hard,
and back again,
as the moment requires:

this is life
and the living
of it. The surviving.

ALWAYS

Always you
until
there is
no more
always.

THE WINGS OF THE WOUNDED

I have wounded myself
so many times, the sharpened edges
I have used
have formed wings
sprouting in shining majesty
from my sweat-streaked back.

They are too heavy
to give me flight,
and if I look at them
the reflected sun
blinds me, even
at night.

And still I add to them,
as years follow years,
as flesh gives ways to wounds
and wounds give way to scars;
there will come a morning,
with their weight
greater than gravity,
when I will be unable to rise
from my bloodied bed,
and any shine
will be absent from their width,
light fading from my gaze.

THIS
    for A

Into your loneliness
we place our voices,
hoping our words
might comfort your wounded heart.

We do not mean
to remind you
of all you have lost
by extolling the manifold virtues
of your husband
now gone, but we are foolish
in the face of grief,
never knowing whether
to share our own
or simply listen to yours.

In truth, we know, without knowing,
there is nothing we can do,
nothing better, nothing worse;
grief spreads its wings
and only flies
when it is ready to fly,

and it will fly,
it will spread itself
across the sky,

9

becoming a gentler being in your world,
lighter and more forgiving.

It will, it will.
This much I know.
This much, at least,
I can give you.

REGRETS

First breaths
and last breaths,
the life lived in-between
peppered with regrets,

so many regrets,

so many, it's a wonder
we have time
to breathe
at all.

ONCE BRIGHT

Conscience is eased
by closed eyes
and sealed mouths,
so much so
the whole world
is willingly becoming blind,
while silence eats away
the faded corners
of our once bright souls.

THE WORDS IN YOUR VOICE

You used to read to me,
I just remembered now
without having that memory
in my head
for I don't know how long,
though rarely has a month passed
without some thought of you.

*Winnie the Pooh, The Lion, the Witch
and the Wardrobe,*
others maybe,
this resurfacing memory
not containing their names.

How I felt,
I do remember,
pure joy and gentle contentment,
my head on your lap,
eyes closed,
the book in one
of your hands,
my hair entwined
inside the fingers
of the other,

and the words,
those magical words

rising and falling
from your mouth,
gentle as the caresses
of the first-time lovers
we almost were,

a piece of a heaven
I believed in then
but believe in no more,
making me smile
as I remember it now;
if we still spoke
I would thank you
for that, yes,
I would thank you,
and smile, at the memory, of course,
but also at seeing you
after all these years.

CRACKED

Who hasn't,
at least once in their life,
looked in a cracked mirror,
only to realise
the mirror is smooth,
their hand already in motion
to touch the cracks
before noticing the truth,
before seeing their face fall
from sight, the vision of their eyes
the last thing to go, the shock
on their face remaining in the air
like a shimmer of heat
on a hot summer's day?

THROUGH

The imprint
of your teeth
has long since vanished
from my skin,
but I still feel
the impact of your passion
vibrating through
my bones,
a music of sorts,
silent, yes, but
still very much there.

TWO COUNTRIES

In the country
that lives in the marrow of my bones
I am a free man,
prone to daydreams
and gentle lies,

while in the country
that beats beneath my steps,
I am a man bound
by all the tales
I have told,
and the tales to come,
those that I must tell
for their ancestral untruths
to remain alive
and true.

ALL I SEE

Dressed as you are
in nothing but morning light,
my breath catches
in my chest, your hand
reaching to pull me near.

PASSION

The collision of our bodies
stills the turning
of the world.

UNWRITTEN POSTCARD

Wish you were here,
but you're not,
nor will you ever be,
here, or anywhere.

I miss you.
I hope you know that.
I would write it down,
but, even if I could gather the words
to contain the uncontainable,
where would I send it?
You no longer exist
to have an address.

You no longer exist,
and I miss you,
my tears staining this postcard
I bought six days
before your funeral.

I AM TOLD

I am told
that love exists
only in the brain,
the heart holding
no claim to its creation,
and yet, as I lay
eyes on you,
it is my heart
that races and rises
in my chest, its eager rush
squeezing the air
from my lungs,
my brain unable
to hold a single thought,
let alone all this love.

FOREVER SPOKEN

Your name
has not passed my lips
in years, but
in the chambers
of my heart
it is forever spoken,
no pause in-between.

WEAKER APART

All our failures
are different,
for the most part,
yet the way
they stain our skins
is always the same.

You'd think we'd recognise
each other, embrace as sisters,
as brothers, united in our missteps,

but we don't,
the failure of others
too much a reminder
of our own failures, and
all the more reason
to succeed on our own.

A WOUND

Don't we all,
somewhere in our hearts,
have a wound
that will not heal?

THIS HOUSE WE BUILD

This house we built
still has some
unfurnished rooms,
like secrets we know are there
but do not need to know,

and we keep building
with every kiss
and tender touch,
every silent moment
of contentment
as we lie beside each other at night,
not needing to be anywhere else
but in this house
we have built
around ourselves,
rooms both unfurnished
and furnished, secrets both
silent and known.

ALL THAT IS GONE

I rarely feel lonely
during the day anymore,
nor even when the night comes
to claim its hours,
but, when I sleep,
oh, when I sleep,
that is when
I dream of you
and loneliness comes upon me
like a wave of oily blackness
as I am reminded
of all that is gone
from me now.

BETTER LIVING THROUGH FOLDING

The news makes more gentle sense
when you fold the paper
into little people,
father, mother,
child, even a dog,
if you fold well.

Stocks land across deaths,
cartoons split through TV listings,
crosswords sever cross words,
meaning diluted, weakened,
unraveled.

One can even lessen
the torment of the outside world,
decrease the potential despair
inherent in all tomorrows,
cruel echoes of today
ever spiraling.

Look, see this paper family,
full of all the world's woes
and TV repeats,
yet they seem happy,
content, unaware
of the doom written across them,
blissful in their blindness.

A STAR

I imagine,
long after
we are both gone,
our love will still shine,
a star in the sky
for new lovers
to wish upon.

BULLY

Speaking as the boy
who was bullied,
mercilessly, for years,
in the indifferent playground
and the darkened school hallways,
the boy you don't quite remember,
there are memories
that never leave
nor heal.

There is knowledge too,
that those who bullied
never give another thought
to the scars they made
in others, and if questioned
might reply with a decisive explanation
of just being kids, children,
not knowing any better,
as though cruelty
must be taught out of the body,
out of the mind.

It doesn't seem fair,
does it, this distance
they allow themselves,
while we, the one's bullied,
those forgotten yet doomed

to always remember,
can never get far away enough
from what we eventually believe
worthy of ridicule
in ourselves.

UNREAD

Every morning I wake
and see the book
you were reading
on the bedside locker,
the bookmark roughly
halfway through,
and I can almost imagine
you returning
to read those remaining pages,
but of course
that is impossible
and those remains pages
will remain forever unread by you

EVEN THIS

Even the memory
of your voice
shaping my name
causes me to smile
all day.

NO SENSE

Even after
all this time
I cannot make sense
of the fact
that when I wake
in the morning
you are gone.

ALL FROM STARDUST

Yes,
we are all born
from stardust,
but you and I
were born
from the same star.

AFTERWARDS

In our house
I walk from
room to room,
expecting to find you
even as I know
you are nowhere
to be found.

BLESSED BE THE UNNAMED

Snow kisses the still body
of the baby
found in the field
days after Christmas,
the baby given no name,
or chance of life,

simply an unknown
left to die
alone in a world
it was brought into
unasked,

yet still a life
and all the possibilities
a life could contain.

MORE

The memory
of my heart
holds every love
I have ever felt,
and, despite everything,
is willing to hold more.

AGED

A hermit crab
has taken my skull
as its own,
scooping out my brain
to fall on the wet sand
of the beach
I used to
wander on
as a child
alive with dreams
and possibilities,
manifold paths stretching before me,

a beach I don't recall
coming to today -
and yet here I am,
somehow - or any day
of my crowded adulthood,
the paths before me fewer,
their surfaces cracked
with weeds one might mistake
for flowers.

OUR EMPTY HOME

Sometimes I forget
that you are gone,
and find myself eager
to tell you about my day
when I reach our empty home.

WAXWORKS

Do you remember that tunnel
in the old waxworks
we crawled though,
stopping halfway through
to kiss, and touch,
our hearts hammering
with desire
and the possibility
of being discovered,
before continuing on,
faces red and bodies eager,
to look at the rest of the wax statues
that looked nothing like
whoever they were meant
to look like, strangers to us
and to themselves?

I remember, of course,
though there is little
I do not remember
of our time together,

our one year, six months
and thirteen days still existing
inside my heart
and nowhere else,
the memory of us

a stranger to you now.

EAGERLY

See my heart
battered and bruised,
new wounds stretched
across old scars,

see it and know
that it will never not beat eagerly
at the possibility of love.

ONCE WE BOTH KNOW PLEASURE

Your cunt spreading
around my dick,
coming home
to come, one
after the other,
or together,
it doesn't matter.

All that does
is having these moments
when we can be
the base beings
we are – purity under
another name – reveling
in the wanting
of each other,

words, panted or otherwise,
no longer needed, both of us
coming, one after the other,
or together, it doesn't matter,

it doesn't matter
once both our bodies know
the pleasure.

WONDERS

It is good
to slow your steps
from time to time,
watch the world
in all its beauty,
appreciate it
and your place
amongst its wonders,
know that you are
a wonder too.

TABLE QUIZ

As questions were asked
that neither of us
tried to know
the answers to,
we touched gentle fingers
beneath the table,
our friends' ignorance of us
a blissful balm upon
the constant risk of discovery,
this pointless table quiz
a viable excuse
to our spouses
to be out together,
alone before everyone.

SMILE

A smile
to a stranger
may be the light they need
to guide them
out of the darkness
their life has become.

THE UNPROVEN POSSIBILITIES OF SPACE

This space above me,
endless, vast,
which I will only ever know
through books and T.V. programmes,
comics and cinema screens,
gives me more comfort
than this earth I lie upon,
this place that is my home
for no other reason than pure chance
and biological circumstance.

This Goldilocks warm planet chills me,
while cold space
generates a warmth in me
as I pour all my sadness into it,
my eyes losing themselves
in its star-pierced darkness

UN-DROWNED

The drowned man
didn't die after
he tried to walk
on the water,
he simply learned
to breathe submerged.

Nor did he cease
trying to walk on water,
now aware that he could not die
in his drowning.

It is a good lesson
to learn, or to know
there is more
than one lesson there;
have any of us
been taking
notes, using quality paper
and ink that won't disappear?

THE HEART OF

You occupy
so much of my heart
it is a wonder
that I can still
call it my own.

(ANOTHER) LOVE POEM

You are all
and everything,
always and forever.

I am more than before,
simply by knowing
the shape of your world.

STILL

Not old enough
to be born, yet
I know your passing
will stretch itself across
the length of my life.

EVEN IN INSOMNIA I KNOW NIGHTMARES

Giving birth to myself
in the sweat
of the night,
I strain to hear a sound
that isn't my own,
some answering voice
to calm my newborn cry,
some gentle words
to mop the nightmare
from my brow.

MY LOVE IS NOT LESS

I knew your body well,
you made sure
of that, our pleasures
always equal
or never felt at all.

It was your heart
you kept a mystery
to me, though
I found enough to love

and continue loving,
even years after
you returned to your husband,
your body always a stranger to him,
though his heart was the home
you sought every night.

YOUR STORM

The news named
the new storm
that was about to lay waste
to a quarter of the world.

It was your name
they used; I couldn't
help but silently nod
in agreement, and
smile too, yes,
smile.

WHAT COULD WE BE WITH WINGS?

I like to imagine
we all have wings
rising from our backs,
invisible, weightless,
none of us knowing
they are there,

and so we never use them,
even as we spend
too much of our lives
looking up at the sky,
sunlight and longing
blurring our eyes,
knowing, without knowing how,
we could be something more,

so much more.

NO PART UNTOUCHED

And the wounds
grief carves
through our heart
never entirely heal,
but we carry on,
we carry on
because we must,
or that grief
will leave no part
of our heart
untouched.

DARKNESS

Before the sky
has bled
all its light,
the streetlights
come on
all at once,
though their growing paleness
seems insignificant
compared to the stubborn sky,
the last of its light
held tightly.

But the sky
must fail, its wound of night
refusing to be healed,
and these streetlights
shall be all that shines,
illuminating the way
for those who need it,

the most insignificant thing
still significant
to someone.

AN IMPOSSIBLE THING

I know
you are gone,
your return
an impossible thing,
and yet I still
search the faces
in a crowd, expecting
to see you smile
as you see me.

FOR YOUR LOVE

My shadow shifts
on the beach
as I stand immobile
searching for a single grain of sand
different from all the rest,

a grain of sand
you asked me to find
before you washed
the all too similar sand
from your skin
in the ever-changing sea,
its cold tide raising goosebumps
on your skin already red
from the sun.

WE PUSH OURSELVES INTO PLEASURE

The flame of a fingertip
parts my skin
as I lie waiting,
eyes blinded
by silk cloth,

and I shudder
in pain and ecstasy,
your mouth suddenly on me
swallowing all that I contain.

THE FIRST OF YOU, THE LAST

Seventy plus years
written deeply
around your eyes,
belie the youth
and mischief
shining in those eyes,

even as you died,
your name a stranger
on your own tongue.

THERE IS A DAY

There is a day
ahead of me,
some possibly distant day,
when the morning
will become the night
and I will have not thought of you.

I do not know,
on that distant day,
if I will smile
or cry. No,
I do not know.

SALT WATER

Salt water
was the only thing
that could ease
his burning heart,
so he said, and
the doctors agreed.

He was found dead
and swollen
to the size of a small island
in the middle of the sea,
either by accident
or design, we shall
never know,

though there were some
who recalled
how he bewailed
the pain in his chest
every time another lover
left him alone, the easing
caused by the salt water
creating a pain of its own.

FAINTLY REALISING

I hoard yesterdays
as though they might aid today
or take some edge
off tomorrow,
faintly realising
I am living less,
all those minutes
and hours
of the past
eating through
the finite time
left before me.

Faintly realising
and yet still gathering them
to me, as though they are warmth
and I am cold to my very bones.

THANKFUL DAYS

There will always
be bad days,
days when it is
hard to smile,
days when it seems impossible
to rise from your bed,

but, there will be
good days too,
days which will scatter
those bad ones aside,
days when you are aware
of the magic
of being alive.

BOY TO MAN

All you taught me,
and I needed
to be taught so much,
I took and gave to others.

I should thank you,
as should they,
the lovers who came after you.

THIS IS MY CHURCH

Saying silent prayers
between your legs
on a Sunday morning
of needing to do
nothing else
but catch your breath hard
in your soft mouth
again and again,
the sound of a day
beginning without us
like a song in the air,
a hymn.

TOGETHER

We walked across the world,
rarely resting, rarely
taking food and water,
simply walked, searching
for a reason
to stay together.

When the world was walked,
our feet broken,
our ankles weak,
we rested and found
when we woke
we needed no reason
to stay together, or
at least not one to be found
by walking the world,
and so we did, stay together,

and still are, together,
the whole world existing
in our shadow.

ALL OR NOT AT ALL

I do not
know how
to love hesitantly.

YOU ARE

You are human,
born of thousands.
There is nothing
you cannot endure.

A FOETAL HEART

As night folds itself
across the sky,
a strange sound fills the air,
like a dog howling backwards,
or a feline retreating out of heat,
and we lie awake
on the bare mattress,
every possibility narrowed
to this point,
as we search
for the second heart
beating inside you,

the beat that was there yesterday
but seems elusive now.

We keep searching
and searching, refusing
to stop and admit
what our own hearts,
beating with a pain
which crowds their constricting chambers,
whisper to us,

whisper so fiercely.

HERE

My arms
will always be
a home for you,

always.

AVOIDANCE

I'm forever boarding trains,
traveling in the wrong direction,
just happy to be going somewhere
that isn't anywhere
I need to be. I am happier
this way, I tell myself
as every explanation I owe
fades into nothing
behind me.

ANOTHER BREAK

My heart has been
rebuilt so many times,
broken pieces reassembled
in the lightless night,
it is barely a heart
anymore. Yet the pain
is always the same,
always, another break,
another piece lost
among the detritus
on the darkened floor.

NEED(LESS)

A different time,
a different place,
we still wouldn't work,
no. It is just
in our bitter natures
to collide until we break,
our attraction to each other
nothing more than
a mockery of need.

IN BLOOD

There were those
who would die,
and did die,
just so we unborn
could be born
in as close to freedom
as we humans
can allow ourselves,
some of their names known,
some forgotten between the gaps
of what the memory of a country can hold.

Now there are those
that get fat off this country,
and stand themselves proud
in the blood of the past,
not realizing the blood was not shed
to stand in, it was shed
to build upon, just as peace
is always built upon war.

AM I FINALLY COMFORTABLE IN MY OWN SKIN?

The warmth I seek at night
no longer comes from you,
but now emanates
from within myself,
some newly discovered chamber
between my stomach
and heart, a place not there
the last time I had cause
to search myself.

You can almost hear
the hum of it, as wave
and wave of heat
ripples through me,
a liquid-less river
creating circles
beneath my skin,
that collide gently
with my bones, the marrow shook
and shook again.

Is this what peace is,
the calm of an untroubled heart?
Is this self-reliance,
the name I reach for
in the mornings now my own?
So many decades

on the planet, I finally
need no longer seek comfort
in the skins of others.

Am I finally comfortable
in my own skin?

YOUR VAST ABSENCE

Your absence
is so vast
I cannot help
but wonder
how it does not
swallow the world.

TO SUFFER A NIGHTMARE ALONE

A pinprick of red light,
flashing on, off,
at the very limit
of my vision,
is helping me fight slumber
as I sit at the curtain-less window,
waiting for the night
to become day,
for no other reason
than with our bed
no longer ours
I would rather not risk sleep
and the dreams
that shake me awake,
crying for safety,
with you not there
to anchor me
in the drowning panic
of those first few seconds
of confused wakefulness.

I smell the ghost
of your cigarettes,
that smell I never liked,
nor the chewing gum that always failed
to hide their taint,
and find myself imagining

that flashing light
at the limit of my vision
could be the tip of a cigarette
smoked by some distant stranger watching me,
as I attempt to not miss you
and the taste of cigarettes and chewing gum
on your tongue.

CONSUMED

Grief consumes my heart,
a cancer devastating
all in its indifferent path,

almost a kissing cousin
to the cancer
that took you from me,
savage and swiftly.

IN DREAMS

We still meet
in dreams, and
I would gladly sleep
the rest of my life away.

(IN)FINITE

I know,
in a life
of finite time,
there is no forever,
and yet, I also know,
that is how long
our love will last.

THE EDGE OF AN ENDING

A lifetime
of biting our tongues
has left half the world mute,
while the other half
says so little in so much
we stopped hearing
their words
a decade, or more, ago,

and then we wonder
why we are here
at the edge of an ending,
the glittered edges slowly
falling away.

ALLOWED

It was only
a matter of time
before he vomited,
drunk as he was
with the sky below him,
the ground above.

They bottled his vomit
after he died, a bottle
blown by the makers
of stained-glass masterpieces,
knowing they could
dilute it to last forever
with the rain that rarely ceased falling,
charge the believers
by the litre,

rebuild their town
that the drunken prophet
had turned upside down
for no other reason
than he was allowed.

THE WEIGHT OF YOUR GOODBYE

Every night
I hear my bones break
beneath the weight
of your goodbye.

BREAK

For so long
I believed
that things broke
as they fell against you.

But time and distance
and a heart almost healed
have taught me
you sought them out
to break, pushed them
when I was not looking,
the crash drawing my eyes
to the shattered remains surrounding you.

It is how me met,
after all, a collision
in a noisy bar, splintered glass shining,
spilled alcohol staining,
followed by a sudden silence
only our suddenly speeding hearts
could fill.

It is how we ended too,
though the noise this time
came from our screams,
the shattered remains mine.

A LOVE WITHOUT PAIN

I have been wrong
about love before,
and I may be wrong
about love again,
but short of never seeking love
I have to risk being wrong
so someday I might finally know
a love without pain.

CHEMOTHERAPY

He stops, the razor
halfway down
his foamed cheek,
and wonders why
he's bothering
with this submission to appearance.

He finds his answer silently,
and finishes his shave,
the razor continuing to his skull,
taking the hair
that remains there,
smiling to himself
at this small victory.

I SEE YOU

I watch as my shadow
pulls away from me
and the sky becomes
my world, the clouds the ground
my feet can barely touch.

Eventually I reclaim
my equilibrium
and risk another glance
at you, the spin beginning
again, the dizziness
like a flutter in my chest.

STILL, STILL

Sometimes,
at night, I hear
all the heartbeats
in the world,
and wonder
how I can be still
so lonely, still so alone.

SPIN

She said he said
this, but he said
she said that,
while he said
and she said,
and no one listened
to all that was said,
only bits and pieces,
full sentences
chopped down
to shapes and sizes
that fit what he said
she said, but what
she didn't say
at all,

and then she did the same
to what he said,
or didn't say,
or didn't mean,
or meant
but not in that meaning,

and we all listened
and heard
what we wanted to hear,
our minds fully made up

with only half the information
and a quarter
of what was said,

making our beds
with unlaundered sheets,
eventually finding all the words
when we complain
this isn't what we wanted,

no, this isn't what we wanted
at all,
no,

listen while we will tell you.

IF ALL

If all I have
left of you
is the memory
of my name
shaped by your mouth,
then that may be enough
for me to survive
your absence from my life.

DIRT

Eating the dirt
from your grave
in some vague hope
of tasting some
memory of you,
makes perfect sense to me
three weeks
after your funeral.

I fear grief and anger
have coiled and cancered
into something approaching madness,

another reason
I cannot live
without you.

WHAT IS SAID

Some say
life is beautiful
because we eventually die,
but I believe
life is beautiful
because knowing we will someday die
we still try to live.

FADING AS YOU FADED

My body is less
without yours beside it,
my chest sunken,
my heart weakened,
my skin taunt across
my thinning bones.

And that smell,
that smell of decay
that emanates
from my flesh,
my body finally succumbing
in sympathy
with yours.

Is that dirt
I taste
upon my breath?

LESSON

Let it hurt,
then let it go.

AN END
for PW

And that is it,
isn't it, your life ends,
but our lives continue on,
days falling into nights,
nights renewing into days,
always, even as we wish
for time to slow, stop,
for just a moment, an hour,
a day, some amount
of time so we might catch our breath,
hold it, fall into senselessness,
that the pain of your absence
might recede from our hearts,
that we might know some of the peace
you now know, pain no longer curling
your being, your very soul,
that we might think of you
without tears staining our breath,

that we might grief
without grieving, and smile
without guilt, or regret.

TIGHTLY

Squeeze me tight,
I am only fragile
when not in your arms.

REMEMBER

Illness made him an echo
of himself
before death made him
a heavy memory
that time and distance made light,
light enough
to rise high
to the back of our minds,
and lie there
waiting to be remembered
with some fondness.

Not his fault
to be remembered as such.
That blame lies clearly with us,
too eager surviving
to spend time remembering
a death that made us realise
we weren't living at all.

FROM THE BEGINNING

Coating the soles
of my feet,
is the soil
I will be buried in.

It comforts me,
knowing it is there,
its grains and lumps,
its damp warmth.

It comforts me, too,
knowing everyone has some
touching the soles
of their feet, present
since birth, though
they are too busy
to feel its touch, its permanence,
too busy moving
so they might live,
too busy living
so they never stop,

never stop
and feel
the soil on their soles,
and the gentle comfort it brings,
the surety of what comes

no matter the steps taken.

SURETY

No, we can never
be sure the sun
will rise tomorrow,
but we can hope,
we can dream,
we can live.

YOUR NAME DEEP

My wounded heart
falls open, your name
scarred deep
into its flesh.

BREATH

Your breath
on the pillow
you've been absent from
for too long
fills me full
with more reasons
to not rise
today.

SO MUCH

So much loneliness
in the world, you
can almost hear it
on the wind, like a sigh
that knows no end.

WE MOVE IN LOVE

Your body
a burning sun
above me. I
am blinded
as I come.

SHE SPEAKS MY NAME

Her silent hand
twists my long hair,
her body arches
into my mouth,
while a language
as old as time
stains her tongue.

I feel her nails
draw blood
and offer her more
of all the lives
contained in our names.

LETTING GO

The words informing me
of your death
sounded absurd
to my ears, as did
the fact you died
two decades ago,
a mere year
after we said goodbye
to a teenage love
I believed would last forever.

I did not believe those words,
cruel lies told by the past
to break the remains
of my teenage heart.
I still do not,
and will not
until I see a body,

until I see you
again.

THIS NEW BREATH

There is nothing
in this world
that I can do
that will ever match
what we have done:

created this life
inside your womb,
for it to develop, grow,
and rush forth,
new lungs roaring
into the world
that will be forever changed
by this new breath
filling the air.

SWOLLEN WITH THE GHOST OF YOU

I miss you
but I no longer
love you, no,
and now there is
a chamber of my heart
swollen with the ghost of you.

HOME

Tasting her
across my tongue
still reminds me
of you, and
it is *your* long fingers
in my short hair
that I feel, pushing
me home.

WITHOUT YOUR SMILE

Yes, the world
will still spin
without you,
but I believe
the sun would shine
a fraction dimmer
without you to smile
into its glow.

BEFORE IT FALLS

Owls talking
across the night
as they hunt for food
to aid their sleep
during the day
is my excuse
for not sleeping
this week, their whispering signature
demanding attention be paid,

another reprieve
from admitting to myself
that you are not coming back
no matter how much sleep I sacrifice,
no matter how many hours I give
to waiting to hear your tread
on the stairs, the reality
a shadow paused before
it falls with all its ungentle fury.

FIRST

Days and nights
have ceased
to exchange themselves,
one for the other,
we have been lying here
so long,

and we are unlikely
to move anytime soon,
our bodies still hungry
for each other, our desire
newborn strong.

TOES

Though I imagine
they would pinch my toes,
I would wear your favorite shoes
to better understand you -
everything else has failed.

But seeing as you were wearing them
when you left me,
that is another possibility
closed to me.

I know your absence though,
from the tips of my toes
to the worn edges of my heart,

I know your absence,
and the pain contained
within its heavy nothingness.

BEATING ANEW

Love changes
every time
it is felt, just as
we are changed
by every love
we feel, our hearts
forever learning
to beat anew.

OUR

I lip-read our future
across your nipples,
my tongue moistening
those words that catch
in your shuddering mouth
as you guide me lower,
deeper.

A LIFE LIVED

You died with a thousand promises
unfulfilled, another thousand
never made, more,
and yet I know
you were happy
with your lot,
with the breaths you were given,
the time you passed
doing what needed doing,

even, sometimes, doing
what didn't need to be done,
and everything in-between.

That is a life,
you would say,
if asked. That
is a life lived.

PALE RIVERS

My scars speak
for themselves,
speak for me,
as most scars do,
the different stories
they can tell
to different eyes.

That is why I keep them covered,
long sleeves and fat watches,
the truth they reveal – the many truths,
some of them even true –
a truth I will not give
to strangers, or friends
for that matter – I have even ceased
seeking lovers, those swift easers
of loneliness, the change in their eyes
as they see them more than I can endure – my eons
of weakness an embarrassment
I would rather not have examined,
the answers required for the questions
that would be forthcoming
not truly shapable by any words I know,
the only comprehensible explanation I could give
being the scars themselves, and perhaps
the shake of my hands as I display their paleness,
like rivers on a map of nowhere.

UNFORTUNATELY

Some people
are a waste
of the stardust
that burns inside them.

IF NEEDED

The fact
that it will end
is reason enough
to embrace
all that a life
can give.

ALIVE

The glass breath of winter
caresses my cheek,
as the idea of snow
hangs in the sky,

and my gloved hand
in yours, this evening walk
across crackling grass,
our daughter before us,
unhesitatingly alive to the world.

Such heaven to be found
in moments
like this.

YOUR SMILE

Your smile
is proof
we all come
from stardust.

MYSELF AS ENEMY

I seek asylum
from myself, but
where can I go
that does not involve
walking across
the broken borders of alcohol,
or the splintered languages of medication?

Where can I go
to escape the madness
of myself, the crashing destruction
of my mind, the taste
of blood in my dreaming mouth?

Where can I go
when there is nowhere to go
but outside of myself,
permanently out,
leaving the little good
I know behind forever,
becoming the enemy
I have always known myself to be?

YEARS

Years since
you have been gone,
and yet you are still
my first thought
when I wake
in the morning.

NO MORE WOUNDS

Aren't we all
just trying
to get through our days
without adding any more wounds
to our souls?

AS VAST

Now that you are gone,
your side of the bed
is as vast
as the curve
of the world.

EYES FOREVER CLOSED

If I close my eyes
I can see you
before me;

I may never open
my eyes
again,

never again.

DESTINATION

I miss watching you,
your fingers leading you
to your desire,
while I stood above you,
my hand equally eager,
both of us aiming
for a merging destination,
sometimes succeeding,
sometimes failing,
neither of us ceasing
until our endings were reached
with fierce cries hard
in our throats.

YOU ARE EVERYWHERE

No matter
how hard I try
I cannot find a memory
that does not involve you.

DREAMS OF YOU

Hard to wake
into your absence
when my dreams
are still so full of you.

ONE LAST TIME

At night
I speak into your side
of the bed, knowing
there will be no reply
from that vast emptiness
and yet, still hopeful
that I might hear my name
shaped by your voice
one last time.

CRUEL

It seems to be
the cruellest trick
a heart can weave,
when the love who left
still appears
in your dreams.

FADED

Years have faded it,
but you can still see
your name
written across
my heart.

NIGHT

We fall
into the night,
our bodies both
soft and hard,
and the morning
is hours away,
hours.

MORE

I melt into you,
my back arched,
my skin shining,
and you take
all of me,
all of me,

and ask for more.

ALL I SEE

You are all
I ever see,
even when
we are not
in the same room.

AN ENDING IS NOT AN ENDING

When the end comes,
as endings must come,
your last breath
will leave your lungs
and enter the world,
a part of you
to last forever.

LIVE, LIVE

Life is too short
to only half-live.

Edward Lee is a poet, writer, playwright and screenwriter from Ireland. His previous poetry collections are *Playing Poohsticks On Ha'Penny Bridge* and *The Madness Of Qwerty*. He is also an accomplished painter and photographer with several of his works in private collections.
When not writing he makes musical noise under the names *Lego Figures Fighting, Orson Carroll, Ayahuasca Collective* and *Pale Blond Boy,* all of which can be found on most streaming services.

His written work can be followed online at:
Instagram: @edwardleepoetry
Facebook: facebook.com/edwardleewriter
Twitter: @PoetryEdward

Printed in Great Britain
by Amazon

36571210R00079